JACKIE JOYNER-KERSEE
RUNNING FOR THE GOLD
Connecting Kids to Dreams

JACKIE JOYNER-KERSEE
RUNNING FOR THE GOLD
Connecting Kids to Dreams

Written by Jackie Joyner-Kersee with Laval W. Belle

Illustrations by Christopher White with Glara Demesmin

Noahs Ark Publishing Service
Beverly Hills, California

Jackie Joyner-Kersee Running for the Gold: Connecting Kids to Dreams
ISBN 978-1-7357447-9-7

Published by:

Noahs Ark Publishing Service
8549 Wilshire Blvd., Suite 1442
Beverly Hills, CA 90211
www.noahsarkpublishing.com

Illustrations by Christopher White with Glara Demesmin

To All Children Around the World

Hi, MY NAME is JACKIE JOYNER-KERSEE,

but you can call me Ms. Jackie. I am the winner of six Olympic medals, three of them are gold.

Today I want to share with you 10 secret treasures on how I won my medals. I keep them hidden here in my dream box.

JACKIE'S DREAM BOX.

INSPIRATION

The first treasure I want to share with you is inspiration. Inspiration is the magic force that creates your dreams and wishes. We get inspiration from movies, books, family and friends. My greatest inspiration is from

ABOVE

DEDICATION

is the time you spend creating dreams. Dreams of acting, sports, singing and learning. Dedication is the power I use to overcome injuries while breaking Olympic

WORLD RECORDS

PRACTICE

is an exercise performed over and over again. Practice is counting numbers, spelling words or rehearsing a play. Practice is learning good lessons everyday. Let's practice

WINNING

DETERMINATION

When days are dark and you want to quit. Determination's sunlight will give you a lift. When dreams seem like nightmares, so far away. Determination like glasses will help you find

YOUR WAY.

GIVING

is sharing with family and friends. Toys, clothes, at parks and gyms. Sharing love, hugs and joy are fine. Giving is doing your best **ALL THE TIME.**

COURAGE

is the treasure that overcomes sickness. While running for the gold around the world, Courage gave me the strength

TO BEAT ASTHMA.

PASSION

is a strong feeling of love, happiness and power. Passion is the electricity that energizes a superhero. Passion is what singers, dancers and athletes use

TO PERFORM.

WHAT iS YOUR PASSION?

NUTRITION

is the food that makes you grow. Foods like fruits, vegetables, water and more. Nutrition gives you energy to run, climb and glow. Nutrition is the juice that makes

YOU GO!

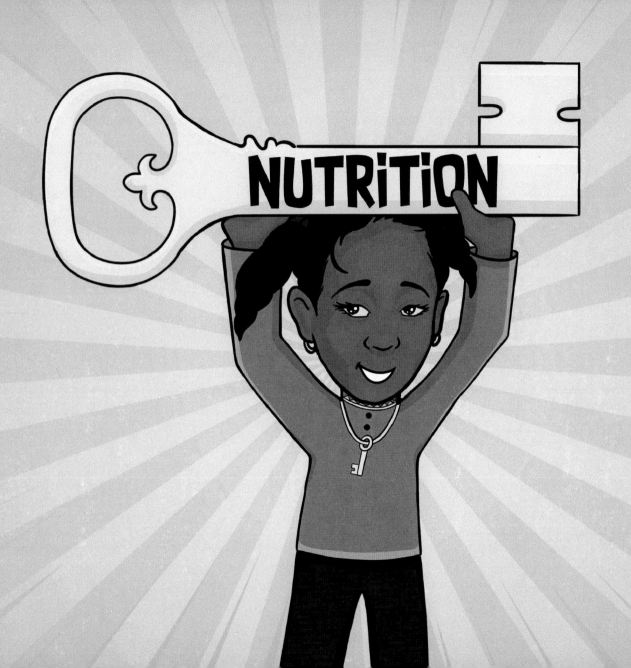

FEAR is being afraid of the dark. Having bad dreams and feeling you are not smart. A monster movie or a doctor's shot. Just be brave and **DON'T YOU STOP!**

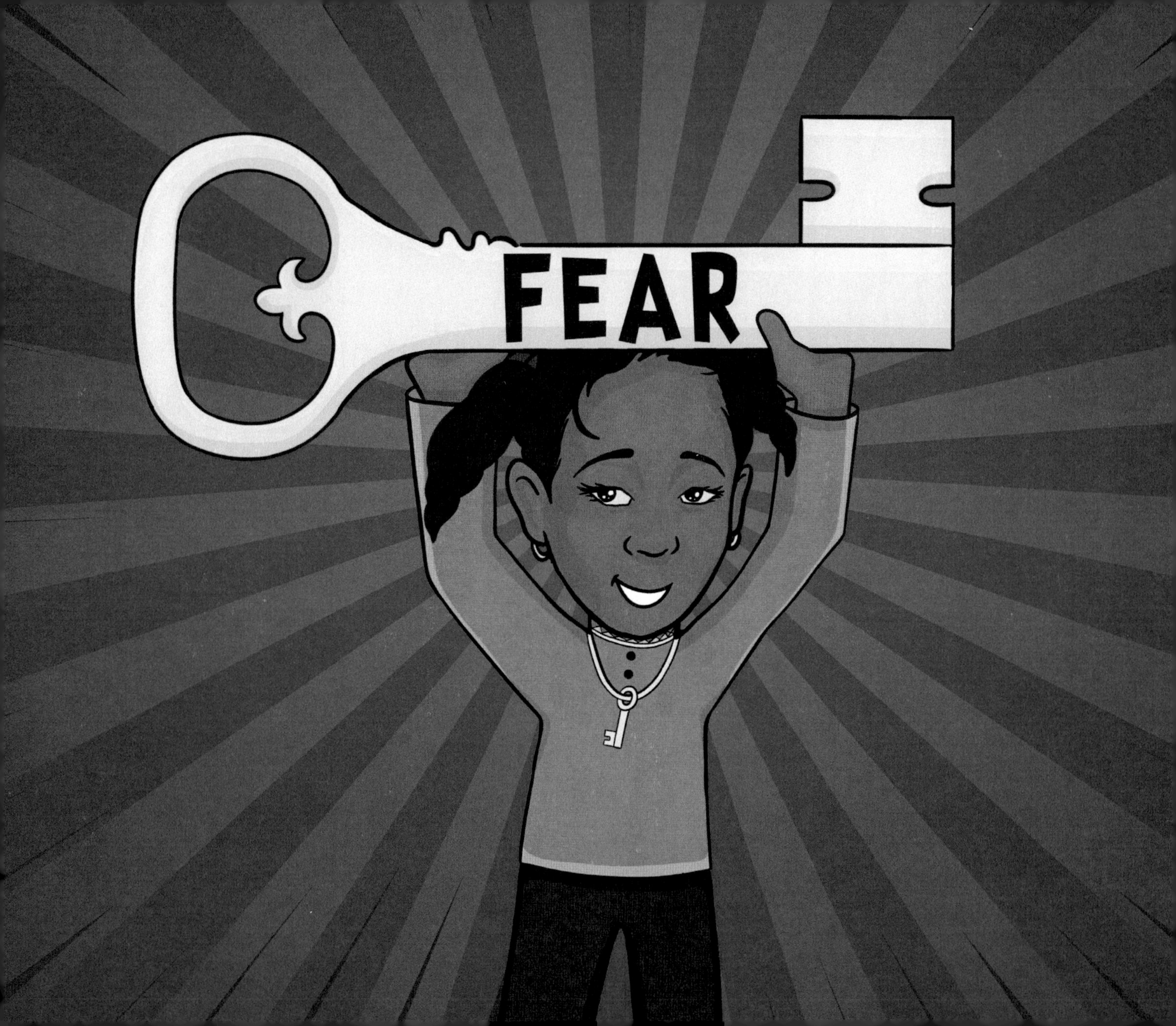
FEAR

FUN

is the treasure that keeps you young. Fun is dancing, singing and playing the drums. Fun is loving family, coaches and friends. Fun makes treasure keys worth doing over and over

AGAIN

For Speaking Engagements, Book Signings, Appearances, and Interviews,

Contact:
Noahs Ark Publishing Service
8549 Wilshire Blvd., Suite 1442
Beverly Hills, CA 90211

Email:
noahsarkpublishing@gmail.com

Phone:
(213) 884-8034

Website:
www.noahsarkpublishing.com

Made in the USA
Monee, IL
31 January 2023

25942794R10019